TOP SCORE MATH
EXTREME SPORTS FACTS AND STATS

XTREME!

By Mark Woods and Ruth Owen

Gareth Stevens
Publishing

XTREME!

By Mark Woods and Ruth Owen

Gareth Stevens
Publishing

Please visit our Web site, www.garethstevens.com. For a free color catalog of all our high-quality books, call toll free 1-800-542-2595 or fax 1-877-542-2596.

Library of Congress Cataloging-in-Publication Data

Woods, Mark, 1972-
Xtreme! Extreme sports facts and stats / Mark Woods and Ruth Owen.
   p. cm. — (Top score math)
ISBN 978-1-4339-5020-9 (lib. bdg.)
1. Extreme sports—Juvenile literature. 2. Extreme sports—Mathematics—Juvenile literature.
I. Owen, Ruth, 1967- II. Title.
GV749.7.W66 2011
796.04'6—dc22

                              2010029612

Published in 2011 by
Gareth Stevens Publishing
111 East 14th Street, Suite 349
New York, NY 10003

© Ruby Tuesday Books Limited 2010

Developed & Created by Ruby Tuesday Books Ltd

Project Director – Ruth Owen
Designer – Alix Wood
Editor – Ben Hubbard
Consultants – Sally Smith, Hilary Koll, and Steve Mills

Images: Getty 7 (Jeff Kardas), 8 (Getty Images Sport), 16 top (Adrian Dennis),
16 bottom (Doug Pensinger), 18 (Christian Pondella), 20 (Jeanne Rice), 21 (Tom Hauck),
22 top (Amanda Edwards), 22 bottom (Carl De Souza), 29 (Heinz Kluetmeier).
Steven Hahn front cover, 12. Shutterstock title page, 6, 10–11 all, 13, 14–15 all,
24–25 all, 26, 27, 28. Wikipedia (public domain) 9, 17, 19.

While every effort has been made to secure permission to use copyright material, the publishers apologize for any errors or omissions in the above list and would be grateful for notification of any corrections to be included in subsequent editions.

Printed in the United States of America

CPSIA compliance information: Batch #CW11GS: For further information contact Gareth Stevens, New York, New York at 1-800-542-2595.

CONTENTS

WARNING!

The extreme stunts and tricks shown in this book have been performed by highly trained sports people. If you want to try them, find out where to get proper training in your area. Do not try them at home!

Neither the publisher nor the authors shall be liable for any bodily harm or damage to property that may happen as a result of trying the tricks in this book.

EXTREME NUMBERS

Extreme sports are all about pushing ourselves to the limit. How high can we go? How far can we travel? How fast can we go? But how do we calculate how far to push ourselves?

By doing the math, we can work it out – whether we are on two wheels, four wheels, on land, in the air, or on water.

Numbers help us plan what we can achieve. They also help us record what we accomplish so that next time, we can try to do something even more amazing. In extreme sports, the numbers count.

Extreme sports stars practice for hours to be the best. It's the same with numbers. When we practice our math skills, we get better and better.

American surfer Kelly Slater is a surfing legend! He has been world champion a record nine times. Kelly used to play in a band called The Surfers and had his own video game about surfing.

To go extreme, we need special equipment such as bikes, parachutes, boards, life jackets, and helmets. The people who design this equipment carefully do their sums to make sure it is as safe and strong as possible. This can mean solving very difficult math problems to make sure we get a thrill!

Motocross champion Ricky Carmichael performs a "can-can" over the head of another racer on the way to winning a race.

Let's get started!

e have always wanted to try new things or be
t to attempt something dangerous or amazing.
re some cool, record-breaking stunts from history.

4, skateboarder
y Way jumped the
d-breaking distance of
et at the X Games.

79

*Danny Way rolls into
one of his Great
Wall of China jumps.*

5

In 2005, Danny Way
jumped over the Great
Wall of China five times.
During one of the jumps,
he covered a distance
of over 60.5 feet.

60

102,800

American pilot Joseph Kittinger holds the record for the highest-ever parachute jump. He set the record in 1960. He was doing tests to find out if astronauts and pilots could survive if they had to escape from a plane or spacecraft high above Earth. Kittinger jumped from a balloon 102,800 feet above the ground (seen here).

RECORD BREAKERS QUIZ

Look at the numbers in the red circles, then try these quiz questions that use those numbers.

1) Joseph Kittinger made a parachute jump from 102,800 feet. What is the value of the bold number?
a) 102,**8**00   b) 10**2**,800

2) Can you write the number **102,800** in words?

3) Try filling the gaps in these number patterns. Each one begins with one of Danny Way's record-breaking numbers.
a) **5   15   ?   35   45   ?   65**
b) **79   85   90   ?   97   ?   100**
c) **60.5   60.75   ?   61.25   61.5   ?   62**

4) Try these calculations using Danny's numbers.
a) **60.5 + 79 =**   b) **60.5 + 60.5 =**
c) **5 x 60.5 =**   d) **5 – 60.5 =**
e) **79 ÷ 5 =**   f) **60.5 – 79 =**

5) Joseph Kittinger fell for 4 minutes 36 seconds before he opened his parachute. Then he parachuted down for 9 minutes 9 seconds. How long was his record-breaking jump in total?

WATER THRILLS

Some extreme sports people get their thrills on water. Surfers look as if their feet are stuck to their boards as they move over and under giant waves. Windsurfers move fast across the water using just a board and sail.

a)   b)

**SURFING
Maximum speed:
35 mph**

In 2006, British surfer Steve King surfed for an amazing 7.6 miles along the River Severn. He was surfing on a large wave called the Severn Bore.

The most famous surfing trick is tubing. A surfer rides under a wave as it turns over.

SURFBOARD STYLE

c)   d)   e)

The world's best windsurfers take part in the Olympic Games every four years. There are speed races and challenges to do the most incredible tricks or ride the biggest waves. Judges decide who is the winner.

**WINDSURFING
Maximum speed:
57 mph**

WATER THRILLS QUIZ

Now try these fun quiz questions.

1) Look at the **Surfboard Style** box. Which of the surfboard patterns has a line of symmetry?

Look at these triangular windsurfer sails.

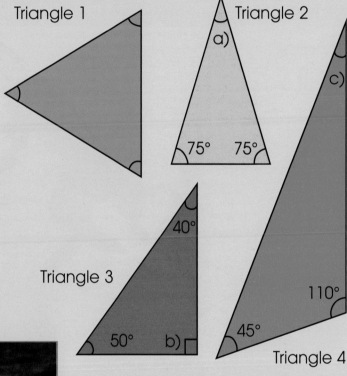

Triangle 1

Triangle 2
a)
75°   75°
c)

Triangle 3
40°
50°   b)
45°   110°
Triangle 4

2) Can you name the four triangles?

3) What is the size of each angle in Triangle 1?

4) Now fill in the missing angles on Triangles 2, 3, and 4.

5) What distance could a windsurfer travel in 30 minutes if she was traveling at 57 mph?

WAKEBOARDING

Wakeboarders strap their feet to a small foam board and are then pulled along by a speedboat while they perform spins, flips, and other tricks. Riders use the waves made by the boat to launch themselves into the air.

Dallas Friday in action

Wakeboarder
American

- Dallas was a competitive gymnast for five years before she began wakeboarding.

- Dallas began competitive wakeboarding when she was 13.

- In 2001, Dallas won the Wakeboard World Cup. She was 15 years old.

- In 2004, Dallas became the first wakeboarder to win an ESPY (Excellence in Sports Performance Yearly) award.

WAKEBOARDING COMPETITIONS

Each rider performs a routine. Three judges give the riders marks in the following categories:

- **Execution:** how well each trick is performed.
- **Intensity:** how difficult the tricks are and how high they are performed.
- **Composition:** the creativity of the rider's routine.

WAKEBOARDING QUIZ

Try these wakeboarding quiz questions.

Dallas Friday is competing in a wakeboarding competition. Each judge awards Dallas a total out of 100.

	Points awarded		
	JUDGE 1	JUDGE 2	JUDGE 3
Execution	20	22	26
Intensity	29	28	27
Composition	21	22.5	20.5

1) How many points in total did each judge give Dallas?

2) To work out Dallas's final score, we use the mean of the three judges' totals. What is Dallas's mean score?

3) Now work out the mean of these sets of numbers.
   a) **10   15   8   31   16**
   b) **6   8   12   15   20   5**
   c) **30   42   26   50**

Look at the **Wakeboard Competition Course** diagram. Each rider makes two passes along the course performing their routine.

4) What is the total distance each wakeboarder travels?

5) If the speedboat travels at 33 feet per second, how long will the two passes take? Give your answer in minutes and seconds.

A flip is when a rider does a somersault in the air and lands with the wakeboard on the water.

WAKEBOARD COMPETITION COURSE

Course length
1,215 feet

1st pass

Start/End   Start/End

2nd pass

SNOWBOARDING

Snowboarding is a combination of skiing and surfing. Snowboarders can achieve speeds of around 125 mph when moving down a slope.

Shaun White in action in a half-pipe competition (above). Shaun has won many top titles, including Olympic gold medals in 2006 and 2010.

XTREME STAR FACTFILE: Shaun White

**Snowboarder
American**

- Shaun is known as "The Flying Tomato" because of his red hair.
- Shaun started snowboarding when he was six years old.
- At 13, Shaun turned professional (he began earning money from snowboarding).
- Shaun has his own half-pipe in the Rocky Mountains in the U.S.
- Shaun invents snowboarding tricks and has his own line of clothing, boots, and boards.

HALF-PIPE COMPETITIONS

- Snowboarders perform difficult acrobatic tricks in a large half-pipe made from snow.

- Five judges give the snowboarders marks out of 10 for style and presentation and for the difficulty and height of the tricks.

SNOWBOARDING QUIZ

Try these snowboarding quiz questions.

1) Look at this points table for a half-pipe competition. Find each snowboarder's total score.

	Judge 1	Judge 2	Judge 3	Judge 4	Judge 5
Luke	6	5.5	7	6	6.5
Shaun	8.5	9	7	7.5	8.5
Marco	5.5	4	4.5	6	7
Mo	9.5	7	6	8.5	9
Kris	6.5	5	7.5	5	4.5

2) Now put the snowboarders in order from 1st to 5th.

3) Can you fill in the gaps in this table?

	Judge 1	Judge 2	Judge 3	Judge 4	Judge 5	Total
Luke	9		6	6.5	8	35
Shaun	9.5	7	8		9	42
Marco	3	5	5.5	7		25
Mo		8.5	7	6.5	7	37
Kris	5.5	7	6		4.5	29.5

Snowboarding competitions are often held in very cold places. The thermometer is showing a temperature of **–5 degrees Fahrenheit (–5°F)**. That means it's **5°** below zero.

−10° −5° 0° 5° 10° 15° 20° 25° 30° 35° 40°

4) If the temperature goes up by **12°F**, what will the temperature be?

5) What will the temperature on the thermometer be if it changes by the following amounts?
a) **+22°F** b) **–4°F** c) **+3°F** d) **+15°F**

FREESTYLE SKIING

Freestyle skiing is all about performing acrobatics high in the air using special take-off ramps, slopes, half-pipes, and superpipes.

MOGULS

- Skiers ski down a slope covered in bumps. The bumps are up to 4 feet high.
- The skiers use the bumps to perform tricks in the air, such as a 360° spin, a flip, or a Daffy – that's when you jump and do the splits in the air.

Freestyle skier Canadian

XTREME STAR FACTFILE: Sarah Burke

- Sarah started skiing when she was five years old.
- Sarah began competing on moguls when she was 15 years old. Often, she competed against boys and was the only girl in the competition.
- In 2007, Sarah became the first woman to land a 1,080° spin in competition.
- Sarah won gold in the Winter X Games in 2007, 2008, and 2009. The photo shows Sarah with her 2009 gold medal.

AERIALS

- The skier takes off fast from a ramp and rises about 50 feet into the air.
- The skier is in the air for around five seconds performing flips and spins.
- Judges award points for the takeoff, the trick, and the landing.

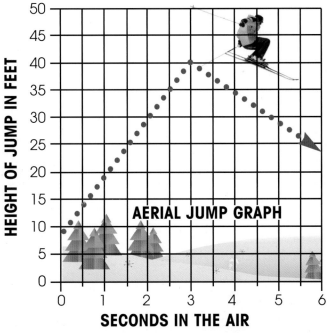

AERIAL JUMP GRAPH

HEIGHT OF JUMP IN FEET

SECONDS IN THE AIR

SPINS AND JUMPS QUIZ

Can you answer these quiz questions about spins and jumps?

1) Freestyle skier Sarah Burke landed a **1,080°** spin.
   a) Divide **1,080** by **10**.
   b) Divide **1,080** by **100**.
   c) Multiply **1,080** by **5**.

2) When something makes a full turn or spin, it goes through 360 degrees.

360°

Look at these freestyle skier spins. How many degrees in each spin?

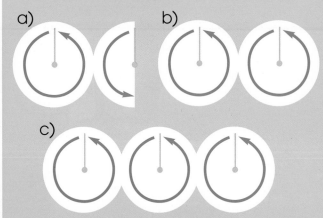

a)

b)

c)

Look at the **Aerial Jump Graph**. It shows a skier during a jump.

3) What height did the skier reach after 2.5 seconds?

4) How long did it take the skier to reach 40 feet high?

5) What height was the skier after 4.5 seconds?

SKATEBOARDING – BIG AIR

Skateboarding is one of the most popular extreme sports in the world. At the X Games, top skateboarders perform amazing tricks and try to get "big air."

Jake Brown competes in the Skateboard Big Air Competition at the 2009 X Games.

SKATEBOARD BIG AIR COMPETITION

- Skaters roll in down a megaramp that can be 79 feet long.
- They are launched over a gap up to 69 feet wide. They pull tricks as they fly over the gap.
- The riders land on a 26-foot-high quarter-pipe and aim to get big air again while pulling another trick.
- Each rider gets five attempts at the jump. Judges award them points for each attempt.

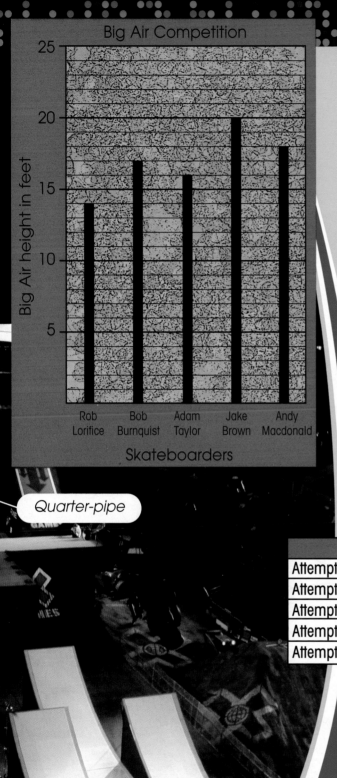

Big Air Competition

Big Air height in feet

25
20
15
10
5

Rob Lorifice | Bob Burnquist | Adam Taylor | Jake Brown | Andy Macdonald

Skateboarders

Quarter-pipe

Try these big air quiz questions.

1) Look at the **Big Air Competition** bar graph.
   a) How high did Jake Brown jump?
   b) Whose highest point was 17 feet?

2) What's the difference between:
   a) Jake's jump and Rob's jump?
   b) Andy's jump and Adam's jump?
   c) Which skaters had a difference of 36 inches?

3) The chart below shows the riders' scores in a big air competition. How many points does each rider have so far? Who has the most points?

	Bob	Jake	Adam	Rob	Andy
Attempt 1	92	80.75	40	55	62.75
Attempt 2	80.5	73	87.5	60.5	68
Attempt 3	70	88.25	90.25	69	72
Attempt 4	50.5	91	62.25	45.5	85.25
Attempt 5					

4) Here are the scores for Attempt 5:
   Bob 80   Adam 78
   Rob 66   Andy 72
   What is the minimum score that Jake can earn on Attempt 5 to be in first place?

5) To work out a rider's final score, we take the mean of his five sets of points. If Jake scores 90 on Attempt 5, what will his mean score be?

SKATEBOARDING – TONY HAWK

Tony Hawk is the most famous extreme sports star in the world. He is an incredible skateboarder and his Playstation game, "Pro Skater," is one of the biggest-selling video games ever.

8

Tony got his first skateboard when he was eight years old. He won his first competition when he was 11 years old. He became a professional skateboarder – one that earns money – when he was 14 years old.

14

11

9

Tony won nine X Games gold medals.

720

Tony says one of his most complicated tricks is the Varial 720-degreer. A varial is when you jump up, spin twice, and then land back on the board.

In 1999, Tony Hawk became the first person to rotate 900° in a skateboard competition. He pulled the trick at the X Games. It took him 12 attempts.

900

12

2.3

Tony's charity, the Tony Hawk Foundation, raises money to build skate parks across the USA. At the start of 2010, it had helped build almost 400 parks at a cost of nearly 2.3 million dollars.

TONY HAWK QUIZ

Now try these quiz questions.

1) How many lines of symmetry do Tony Hawk's initials have?

T   H

Now try finding lines of symmetry in your own initials.

2) Try these questions that use the numbers in the red circles.
   a) What is one quarter of **8**?
   b) Multiply **14** by three.
   c) What number can you add to **11** to make 20?
   d) What is one-sixth of **12**?
   e) What is **900** minus **720**?

3) Tony won nine gold medals for skateboarding. Try these number 9 calculations.
   a) **9 + 9 + 9**   b) **9 x 9**
   c) **99 ÷ 9**   d) **9 – 19**

4) Can you work out the missing numbers in these decimal calculations that include the number **2.3**?

   a) **2.3 +** ☐ **=10**   b) **8.7 –** ☐ **= 2.3**

   c) **2.3 + 2.3 =** ☐   d) ☐ **+ 2.3 = 7.5**

5) Tony made a famous **900°** series of rotations (spins). How many lots of **90°** are there in **900°**? Can you draw a diagram to show Tony's trick? (Look at our diagrams on page 17.)

BMX

BMX is short for bicycle motocross. Two wheels, a track, crazy jumps – and bikes moving at up to 50 mph! The first BMX bikes were built in the 1970s. The sport became popular with kids who built their own jumps to try flying through the air like the motorbike stuntmen they saw on TV.

BMX racing became an Olympic sport in 2008. Anne-Caroline Chausson of France (seen in the lead here) won the women's gold medal.

BMX FREESTYLING

Park: using jumps and obstacles in a specially built park.

Dirt: this takes place on dirt tracks with jumps along the way.

Street: riding outdoor objects such as steps, rails, banks, and curbs.

Vert: using a half-pipe to build up speed and flip the bike in the air.

Flatland: doing tricks on a flat surface using balance to lift the rider and bike into different positions and spins.

BMX PARK

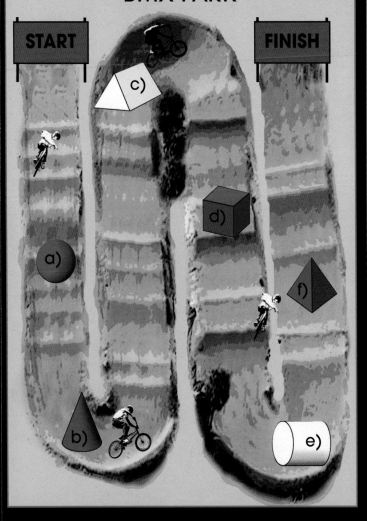

START FINISH

c)
d)
a)
f)
b)
e)

BMX QUIZ

Try these quiz questions about BMX racing and tricks.

1) Mat Hoffman achieved "air" of 50 feet on his bike.
   a) How many inches in 50 feet?
   b) If Mat achieved 50% of that jump, how high would he be?
   c) Put these "air" heights in order starting with the lowest:

14 yd	40 ft	564 in
37 ft	456 in	17 yd

2) Look at the **BMX Park** diagram. Each obstacle is a 3D shape. Can you name each shape?

3) There are eight riders in an Olympic BMX race. If 32 riders enter the competition, how many races will there be in the first round?

4) The fastest four riders from each race go through to the next stage. Look at these race times. They have been timed in seconds. Which four riders went through?

Rider A: **29.5**	Rider B: **28.3**
Rider C: **29.2**	Rider D: **27.7**
Rider E: **28.5**	Rider F: **28.9**
Rider G: **27.9**	Rider H: **29.1**

5) How many tenths of a second faster must **Rider F** go to make the final four?

MOTOCROSS

Motocross riders race special bikes around muddy dirt tracks with huge bumps and steep banks.

MOTOCROSS RACE FACTS

- A track can be 5,000 to 6,500 feet long. The track is cut through a field with plenty of twists, turns, hills, and slopes.
- The bikes can travel at 90 mph.
- Riders must be strong and fit. Races can last for 30 minutes and the track gets rougher as the race goes on.

Motocross bikes are made from lightweight aluminium and tough plastic. They weigh just 220 pounds.

FREESTYLE MOTOCROSS

- Freestyle riders use ramps or natural hills to make giant leaps.
- When the riders are in the air, they perform amazing tricks such as "seat grabs" and backflips.

Answer these quiz questions about motocross racing and tricks.

1) At the start of a motocross race, the starter holds up a 30 seconds board. Then the countdown to the start of the race begins. Try filling in the gaps in these countdowns.
   a) **30 25 ? 15 ? 5**
   b) **30 27 ? 21 ? 15 ?**
   c) **30 20 ? 0 –10 ? –30**

2) Forty riders start a race. Five riders have a crash and pull out. Two riders have mechanical problems and pull out. Six riders get tired and slide off into the mud. How many riders finish the race?

3) If a race lasts 30 minutes and a rider makes 10 laps in that time, how long does each lap last?

4) If a track is 5,000 feet long, how far will a rider travel if he makes five laps of the track?

5) A freestyle rider practices a seat grab 20 times. He gets the trick right four times out of 20.
   a) Show this fact as a fraction in its simplest form.
   b) Show the number of times he missed the trick as a fraction in its simplest form.
   c) If the rider practices the trick 30 times and gets it right 50% of the time, how many perfect seat grabs will he perform?

THRILLS IN THE AIR

Imagine standing on the edge of a plane door and just leaping out into the sky! That's what skydivers do for thrills. Skydivers leap from the plane and freefall towards Earth at around 165 feet per second. Then they pull a special cord on their backpacks, their parachutes open, and they slowly float down to the ground.

SKYDIVE BASICS

- A standard skydive takes place from a height of around 10,000 to 13,000 feet.
- The skydive will last for around seven minutes.
- First-time skydivers jump attached to an instructor who makes sure that everything goes according to plan.

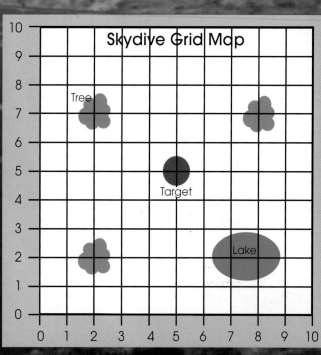

Skydive Grid Map

Tree

Target

Lake

Paragliding starts with the chute already open. Paragliders take off from a mountaintop or the edge of a cliff.

PARAGLIDING RECORDS

- Will Gadd set a record for a paraglider flight in 2002 in Texas. He flew for 262 miles. The flight lasted 10 hours and 38 minutes.

- In 2008, Nevil Hulett from South Africa flew 312 miles– a new record.

Don Kellner, a former U.S. Air Force instructor, has made over 39,000 skydive jumps since 1967. He also helps people take their first skydive.

THRILLS IN THE AIR QUIZ

Try answering these quiz questions about paragliding and skydiving.

1) Look at the **Paragliding Records** information. How much further was Nevil's flight than Will's?

2) You are making a skydive. During freefall, you fall at 164 feet per second. If you freefall for half a minute, how far will you fall?

3) Now use your answer to question 2. If you start your jump at 13,000 feet and are in freefall for half a minute, at what height do you open your parachute?

4) In competitions, skydivers try to land as close as possible to a target spot. The winner is whoever comes nearest. Look at the **Sky Dive Grid Map**. The red circle is the target spot.
   a) Give the coordinates of the target spot.
   b) Where will you be if you land on **(8,2)**?
   c) Where will you be if you land on **(2,7)**?

5) Here are the landing places of some skydivers. Which landing place is nearest to the target?
   (9,4) (6,5) (4,7) (3,5) (6,8) (5,2)

ROCK CLIMBING

Rock climbing is a massive challenge, whether it's on a small indoor climbing wall or a huge mountain. It can be very dangerous and tests a person's strength, balance, and ability to move quickly and easily.

ROCK CLIMBING BASICS

- Climbers find small openings in the rock and use their hands and feet to pull themselves up or across.
- Climbers can be attached to a rope that is fixed firmly into the rock. If they slip, the rope will stop them falling.
- In climbing competitions, climbers race to reach the top of a climbing wall or rock face. Sometimes the competition is to see who can climb a route in the quickest time.

ROCK CLIMBING CHALLENGE

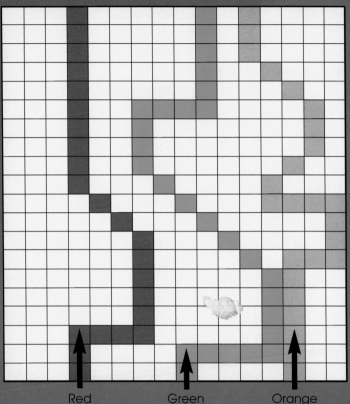

Red climber start   Green climber start   Orange climber start

ROCK CLIMBING QUIZ

Finally, try these quiz questions about rock climbing.

Look at the **Rock Climbing Challenge** diagram. It shows the routes that three climbers took on a rock face. We can describe their routes using compass directions like this:

Red Climber Route

3 squares north
3 squares east
5 squares north
3 squares northwest
9 squares north

1) Describe the green climber's route using compass directions.

2) Describe the orange climber's route using compass directions.

3) If each square on a route is one move, which climber used the fewest moves to reach the top?

4) If each square of a route is worth 30 seconds, how long did it take each climber to reach the top? Give your answer in minutes and seconds.

5) If each square of a route is worth 1.5 yards, what distance did each climber cover on their route?

9 RECORD BREAKERS QUIZ

1 a) 800 b) 2,000
2 One hundred two thousand eight hundred
3 a) 25, 55 b) 94, 99
   c) 61, 61.75
4 a) 139.5 b) 121 c) 302.5
   d) −55.5 e) 15.8 f) −18.5
5 13 minutes 45 seconds

11 WATER THRILLS QUIZ

1 Surfboards a and e have a line of symmetry
2 Triangle 1 – equilateral
   Triangle 2 – isoceles
   Triangle 3 – right-angled scalene
   Triangle 4 – scalene
3 60°
4 a) 30° b) 90° c) 25°
5 28.5 miles

13 WAKEBOARDING QUIZ

1 Judge 1: 70 Judge 2: 72.5
   Judge 3: 73.5
2 72 points
3 a) 16 b) 11 c) 37
4 2,430 feet
5 1 minute and 14 seconds

15 SNOWBOARDING QUIZ

1 Luke 31; Shaun 40.5;
   Marco 27; Mo 40; Kris 28.5
2 1st: Shaun 40.5
   2nd: Mo 40
   3rd: Luke 31
   4th: Kris 28.5
   5th: Marco 27
3 Here's the table with the missing numbers filled in.

	Judge 1	Judge 2	Judge 3	Judge 4	Judge 5	Total
Luke	9	5.5	6	6.5	8	35
Shaun	9.5	7	8	8.5	9	42
Marco	3	5	5.5	7	4.5	25
Mo	8	8.5	7	6.5	7	37
Kris	5.5	7	6	6.5	4.5	29.5

4 +7° Fahrenheit (or 7°F)
5 a) +17°F   b) −9°F
   c) −2°F   d) +10°F

17 SPINS AND JUMPS QUIZ

1 a) 108 b) 10.8 c) 5,400
2 a) 540° b) 720° c) 1,080°
3 35 feet   4 3 seconds
5 33 feet

19 BIG AIR QUIZ

1 a) 20 feet
   b) Bob Burnquist
2 a) 6 feet b) 2 feet
   c) Rob and Bob;
      Jake and Bob
3 Bob 293; Jake 333; Adam 280; Rob 230; Andy 288
   Jake has the most points
4 41 points   5 84.6

21 TONY HAWK QUIZ

1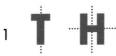

2 a) 2 b) 42 c) 9 d) 2 e) 180
3 a) 27 b) 81 c) 11 d) −10
4 a) 7.7 b) 6.4 c) 4.6 d) 5.2
5 10 lots of 90°; your diagram could look like this:

23 BMX QUIZ

1 a) 600 in b) 25 ft
   c) 37 ft 456 in   40 ft
   14 yd   564 in   17 yd
2 a) Sphere b) Cone
   c) Triangular prism
   d) Cube   e) Cylinder
   f) Square-based pyramid
3 Four races
4 Rider D: 27.7 seconds
   Rider G: 27.9 seconds
   Rider B: 28.3 seconds
   Rider E: 28.5 seconds
5 5 tenths of a second faster (0.5 second faster)

25 MOTOCROSS QUIZ

1 a) 20, 10 b) 24, 18, 12
   c) 10, −20
2 27 riders
3 3 minutes
4 25,000 ft (or 4.73 mi)
5 a) 1/5 b) 4/5 c) 15

27 THRILLS IN THE AIR QUIZ

1 50 miles
2 4,920 feet
3 8,080 feet
4 a) **(5,5)** b) In the lake
   c) In a tree
5 **(6,5)**

29 ROCK CLIMBING QUIZ

1 Green climber route
   2 squares north
   4 squares east
   4 squares north
   6 squares northwest
   3 squares north
   3 squares east
   5 squares north
2 Orange climber route
   7 squares north
   2 squares east
   3 squares north
   3 squares west
   1 square north
   2 squares northeast
   2 squares north
   3 squares northwest
   2 squares north
3 Red climber
4 Red 11 minutes 30 seconds;
   green 13 minutes 30 seconds; orange 12 minutes 30 seconds
5 Red 34.5 yd; green 40.5 yd; orange 37.5 yd

aerial: occurring in the air

aluminum: a soft, white metal

complicated: difficult

coordinate: any of a set of numbers used to tell the location of a point on a grid

diagram: a drawing that shows the arrangement of something

grid: a network of evenly spaced lines running across and up and down

half-pipe: a U-shaped ramp with high sides

helmet: a protective head covering made of hard material

maximum: the greatest quantity or value that can be reached

mechanical: having to do with machines or equipment

minimum: the smallest quantity or value that can be reached

motocross: a type of motorcycle race that uses special motorcycles and takes place on a muddy track with bumps, steep hills, and sharp turns

Olympics: competitions held every four years between the best athletes from countries around the world

parachute: a fabric device used to slow the fall of a person or object

quarter-pipe: one half of a half-pipe

ramp: a sloping surface

rotate: turn or revolve

routine: a worked-out set of tricks to be performed

stuntman: a man who performs difficult feats requiring great skill

superpipe: a large half-pipe

symmetry: the property of matching on either side of a dividing line or around a center